Helping the Hurting

A Guide for People of Faith

Cori Moschberger, MSW, LCSW

Copyright © 2016 by Cori Moschberger.

All rights reserved. No part of this book may be used or reproduced by any means, graphic, electronic, or mechanical, including photocopying, recording, taping or by any information storage retrieval system without the written permission of the copyright holder, except in the case of brief quotations embodied in critical articles or reviews.

ISBN 978-1-890586-54-6 (print)
ISBN 978-1-890586-55-3 (ePub)
ISBN 978-1-890586-56-0 (mobi)

TIPS Technical Publishing, Inc.
108 E. Main Street, Suite 4
Carrboro, NC 27510
www.technicalpublishing.com

Printed and bound in the United States of America

To the loved ones in my life who have walked with me through painful times and to all those who experience hurt in our world and need the presence of a loved one to help them heal

Contents

Introduction   1
   Doubt in Faith   3
   Anger in Hope   5
   Are Doubt and Anger Allowed?   7
Lesson 1: Just Sit   9
Lesson 2: Sit Some More   15
Who's to Blame (And Does It Matter)?   19
   When It's Their Own Fault   19
   When Someone Else Is to Blame   23
Lesson 3: Show Up   29
Lesson 4: Choose Your Words   35
Lesson 5: Speak Hope   41
   Some of God's Promises   43
Final Lesson   49
   In Closing…   51
About the Author   57

Acknowledgments

Special thanks to my editor—who is also my little sister—for believing in me!

Introduction

This book is about how a person of faith can best help the hurting. It is not for counselors or pastors or anyone else in the helping profession. In fact, my advice would be quite different for anyone helping someone in a professional capacity. This book is for the average person who has friends and loved ones going through difficult times. If you are in the helping profession please understand that this applies to your role as a friend, mother/father, sister/brother, daughter/son, etc.

This book is also not about finding solutions or fixing problems, or explaining why God allows hurt in our world. Quite frankly, I have no answers for any of that. In the midst of writing this I am supporting a very dear friend going through what will probably be the most difficult season of her life. My heart is broken for her and my soul aches to fix what I cannot. My questions about why God allows hurt in this world have only grown in supporting her through this experience. It is with this realization that my hand has reached for a pen and paper once again.

The process of writing is often a difficult one for me, as when I am writing I am actually processing instead of avoiding. I'm an excellent avoider, it's my top coping skill and over the years I have mastered it. But I find in avoiding I have to shut myself down emotionally, particularly from God, and I cut off the process of learning and growth. Growth is painful and when I am already experiencing pain in my life or sharing in the pain of someone I love, I am not looking for any more pain; thus my use of avoidance. It is counterproductive—I know this—but it often takes me months to be able to put my hand to the pen (or keys) again. When I finally concede, I find that what I have learned is something I want others to know without having to experience the same pain I have.

My desire in writing this book is to help others learn what I have learned about supporting someone going through a tumultuous time in their lives. I am a Licensed Clinical Social Worker, but most of my writing here will focus on my experience as friend, daughter, and sister. The training I received as a counselor seems to go right out the window when I am helping someone I love and am emotionally involved with.

My first experience with helping the hurting came from actually being supported when going through my own dark hour and later, being the support to someone else. I think as people of faith we often fail miserably at this, offering trite words and quick prayers to someone whose heart is broken and faith is rocked. I believe we most often fail to be a strong support for others because we are afraid of the darkness ourselves: afraid that our own faith will not stand the test, and afraid that we will not be able to fix what is happening in the life of someone we love.

What I know from being the one in the valley is that all we need is the presence of someone who loves us, not the right words or the perfect faith; in fact, that can often be horribly annoying when you have been shaken at your core and someone else seems to say all the right things and leaves no room for doubt in faith. They go hand in hand don't they—doubt and faith? And often anger and hope too.

How do these opposites go together? To me it's like life and death—how do they fit together? They are complete opposites and yet entirely connected. So can you have both—doubt and faith, anger and hope? I believe you can.

Doubt in Faith

What does doubt in faith look like? This is different for everyone but in my experience it is knowing *who* God is, what he has done for you through the death and resurrection of his son, and wondering where he is and how he could allow this circumstance to happen. This is particularly difficult for Christians to admit they feel themselves and it is just as difficult, if not more difficult, to give permission to someone we love to feel this way. We are afraid that our loved one will lose faith all together and turn from the God we love, so we try to grab hold of them tightly and fail to allow the doubt they cannot help but feel.

We think having faith should eliminate the doubt and when it doesn't we are confused and often feel guilty. Jesus said having the faith of a mustard seed could move mountains (Matt. 17:20), and we think, "If I can't even keep the faith when life dumps me upside-down how could I ever have enough faith to move mountains?!" However, I have found that it is in this state that our faith is grown the most. Not in our times of strength, but in our times of weakness and dependence.

So where, in times of weakness, do we go to find faith? For me, faith has become anchored to the character of God remaining consistent and steadfast. Early on in my adult life I went through my first dark valley. At the time, I prayed and prayed that God would step in and change things and all I felt was his absence. I remember talking with a friend about my feelings and asking how I could have faith in prayer when God wasn't answering my prayers. His response was life changing. He said, "You don't need to have faith in prayer, you need to have faith in God." What a change of my worldview! Faith is solely based on *who* God is. Where he is in our circumstance, what he is or is not doing, how he is or is not responding to our prayers—all of that is a fertile breeding ground for doubt and endless questions that ultimately will plague each of our lives at some point. But knowing *who* he is becomes a rock you can stand on when the storm rages all around you. This is doubt *in* faith.

Anger in Hope

Ah, anger in hope; this is a tough one. Clinging to hope when you just cannot find any hope in the circumstances. Anger is the first emotion that comes when life kicks us, not hope. Anger left to fester without hope will lead to despair. But where can hope be found when everything around us seems hopeless? Again, hope is found in the unchanging character of God—not what he is or is not doing, or how he is or is not working, or where he is in our circumstances but in *who* he is.

Hope comes when we know with confidence that he is good. If you have not yet sorted this out for yourself, it will be virtually impossible to help someone else who is in a place of questions and anger.

This was another lesson I learned through that first dark valley of my adult life. When life dumped me out on my head I had to ask myself, "If God is good when things are good is he also good when things are bad"? If the answer was yes I had hope in *who* he is. If the answer was no then the ultimate outcome was hopelessness because I could not depend on the character of God.

At the time this question was rolling around in my head, God gave me a very vivid object lesson through a real-life experience. I was waitressing part time at a small family-owned Italian restaurant and it was exactly as you might imagine it—the husband and wife who owned the restaurant yelling at each other or one of their two sons in the kitchen on most nights.

The chef, Oscar, was responsible for every meal and dessert that went out. So one night, early in the evening, I put in an order for oysters accidentally. Oscar made them for me and, when I confessed my error, told me it was no problem and handled it without telling the owners. Later that same night I placed an order for Bananas Foster (a very yummy dessert). After receiving the order, Oscar told me he was out of bananas and to offer the table something else. The only way for me to change the check was to inform the owner and ask him to remove the Bananas Foster from the ticket. When I asked him to void it for me, he asked me why I needed it voided and I told him Oscar was out of bananas. He promptly went in the kitchen to very loudly scold Oscar for his failure in not ordering enough bananas. When I walked into the kitchen, Oscar sarcastically thanked me for telling on him and asked if I had also told the owner about the oyster order I had messed up earlier. I felt terrible and apologized profusely, explaining that I had no choice because I had to void the dessert and could not do that without the owner. His response would change my view of God forever. He said, "It's okay. It's just that I put out hundreds of perfect meals every night and he says nothing. Then the one time I run out of bananas he's all over me."

It struck me that night on my ride home that this is how we handle God, isn't it? He does endless good in our world and in our lives and we fail to thank him, in fact we fail to even notice in most cases. But the second something goes wrong, we are all about blaming him aren't we? I began to affectionately call this my "hundreds of bananas" story. It spoke so clearly to me of who God is and how we handle him in our anger while we are searching so desperately for hope.

The knowledge that if God is good when things are good, he must also be good when things are bad or he is not who he says he is did not replace the anger with hope—instead it allowed me anger *in* hope. I felt both. I could rest my hope in the knowledge that God is good—he loves me more than I could ever know, he wants the best for me, and the pain in our world breaks his heart. At the same time, I could be angry at what was happening in my life, angry that God wasn't stepping in in the way I wanted him to or when I wanted him to. This is anger *in* hope.

Are Doubt and Anger Allowed?

Yes! God can handle your doubt and the doubt of your loved one. God can also handle your anger and the anger of your loved one. You can experience faith while you're smack dab in the middle of doubt and you can experience hope when you are plagued with anger. This happens when we know the character of God and bank on the fact that *who* God is doesn't change. He is "the same yesterday, today, and forever" (Heb. 13:8).

But *who* he is doesn't fix the circumstances. *Who* he is doesn't change the fact that your own wrongdoing just landed you in a pit, or that the wrongdoing of someone else just kicked you in the gut, or that we live in a broken world and you just got dropped on your head. It is the what of the circumstances, and the how, and the when, and the why that brings anger and doubt, and quite frankly, there is just no way around that. Give yourself or your loved one permission to feel that. Doubt does not mean the absence of faith and anger does not mean the absence of hope; they coincide with each other in honesty—because if you're honest, you admit that you never feel all positive or all negative: it's always a bit of both and the struggle becomes leaning in to faith and hope when life is dishing out doubt and anger.

Lesson 1: Just Sit

There are some who call this the "Gift of Presence" or "Holding Space." This is where support begins and it is a hard one for many of us; we want to do things, find solutions, help, give answers, etc. But what someone who is hurting needs is someone to just sit with them. Just allow them to hurt. That is painful for us because we love them and want to see them happy, not hurting, but that is not the reality of life. Life brings pain. If it hasn't yet for you, you are either a better avoider than me or it just hasn't happened to you yet, but I can pretty much guarantee that it will. Unfortunately, life is full of pain. At times though, it is more painful to watch someone you love hurting than to deal with pain in your own life. We often wish we could take the pain from those we love; too bad we can't. But we *can* be a salve to the wound, which means we have to take a good hard look at the wound, acknowledge its realness, and hold a gentle cloth to the seeping.

The first part of dealing with pain is the initial shock of the wound. It's debilitating. If you have been there you know what this feels like. To paraphrase a quote from a movie I like, the worst thing about this kind of pain is that it doesn't actually kill you. And you wish it would, don't you? You may even ask for it to kill you because that would be so much easier than living through it. But it doesn't. So now there is this open gaping wound gushing blood. Do you need someone to run around cleaning up the blood and changing the linens or do you need someone to sit with you and help the bleeding stop? Eventually, the blood will need to be cleaned up and the linens will need to be changed but not yet. First we have to help the bleeding subside. We do that by sitting.

What does that mean exactly? This is not a code word, it means exactly what you think it means—sit with your loved one. Maybe they can't get out of bed and you need to be there in your pjs with them snuggled up with tissues and the dog. Maybe they need to watch TV to distract their minds and you need to be on their couch with a great Netflix series. Maybe they need to talk and that is best facilitated with food—could be popcorn on the couch or a meal out in a busy restaurant where they can be anonymous. Maybe they need to go for a walk and just want another body beside them on the trail. The specifics will change for each person but your role remains the same: just be with them.

I know in theory this is simple, but in reality it is very difficult. It means we are not giving any answers, any great pearls of wisdom, any encouraging Bible verses;

we're not praying or talking about our own experience and how we think it relates to theirs; we are just sitting with them in the darkness.

What's the point, you ask? It reminds them they are not alone, and if you can be there with them perhaps God can also handle their darkness and hasn't left them. How important is that?! When you go through the valley, you feel completely isolated and alone and God feels like a giant cosmic being who created the world and set it on its axis without any further involvement. The presence of people who love you is the only way to break that feeling of isolation and abandonment. It is through your presence that you become Jesus with skin on in their life.

I don't know if you have experienced this but I sure have. There are just a few key moments that really stand out to me in the very beginnings of the dark moments in my life when someone loved me enough to just sit with me.

The first was when the darkness was because of someone else and the pain they caused me and a friend came over and lay in bed with me all day while I cried and she just cried with me and held my hand. That was it. It was so significant that more than ten years later I can recall everything about the way my loneliness dissipated that day despite my circumstances.

The second was when the darkness was caused by my own wrongdoing and a friend loved me enough to listen to my confession and not say a word. We sat in her car while I cried and she just listened. She didn't judge me, she didn't condemn me, she didn't give me the okay to stay in my darkness, she just sat with me. Eventually she would actually pull me out of the pit I had dug for myself but not yet. It was in that moment that I thought if she could handle my wrongdoing perhaps God could too. It was the beginning of my path to redemption.

The thing that helps make just sitting with someone in the pain easier is to remember that there really are no words to make it better. We try to use words to make it better because we so desperately want to help those we love, but there are none. Validate their pain—pain sucks! Let's just be honest here. There is no silver lining in the pain. In hindsight we might be lucky enough to catch a glimmer (though I wouldn't count on it) but in the moment there just isn't any—plain and simple. If you absolutely must say something, just say, "I don't know what to say but I love you and I'm here." And please, whatever you do, do NOT throw out any quippy misuses of scripture—like "God won't give you more than you can handle" (not the right application) or "All things work together for good for those who love God" (again, not the right application). Not only are these misused and out of context, they are just plain annoying! Of course God is still sovereign and he is still present and he does have a plan for this person's life but the only way they are going to experience any of *who* God is in this darkness is through your presence, love, and acceptance of them exactly as they are—beaten and bloody and full of doubt and anger. So ditch the words for now and just sit.

Let me also say that although trust is required for this, you don't have to be a person's best friend to sit with them. Because it is all about your presence and not about the amazing things you say that you just know will help them, the only requirement is that you care about this person, and in your empathy, their pain causes you pain. It may be in the sitting that your relationship deepens and becomes a place of authenticity and safety for years to come.

Lesson 2: Sit Some More

*N*o, seriously! We live in a world of "my way, right away" and pain just doesn't work that way. It takes time to heal even when a person has only taken one emotional beating; but what if the emotional beatings continue over the course of months or years? How long will the healing take then? What if there is never "healing"? Again, this is hard for us because we want the people we love to feel better fast, but that is just not the reality of pain.

This is really where the rubber meets the road in helping someone who is hurting. There are a lot of people around when the pain first hits. Think about losing someone to death—there are visits and meals and cards for a few weeks but then, as it must, life goes back to normal for everyone else except the grieving, and they feel like life should go back to normal but they just can't seem to make that happen. It takes time to learn how to live in the "new normal." I think in general, we all hope that things will go back to the way they were before the pain, but they never do—they can't because things are no longer the same. A counselor of mine once told me, "Life is like a book, this chapter may end but it will always be a chapter in the book." We want so badly for the pain to go away, for the ordeal to end, to close the book and put it away for good, but we can't ever go back to what life was before this chapter of pain was added. It's a part of our story now.

Who are the characters in your chapters of pain? That is what makes the difference isn't it? Lyrics from a favorite song say, "You're not alone in this story's pages"—that's the key isn't it? It's the characters who stay by your side through the chapters of pain who make the difference in what the next chapters of life will look like.

I have found that the characters involved in my chapters of pain have changed very little over the course of my adult life, although I must say there are occasionally one or two friends that surprise me by being a support I never expected. These are the friends I would not have considered to be close friends before the pain hit but following their willingness to just sit with me and sit some more I now consider them treasured friends. I can think of three people who played a role in this way during a dark season of my life. We were not close, but they were present with me in my season of pain. Today, they all live across the country from me and we rarely get in touch but there is a special fondness for each of them, a genuine love that fills my heart when I think of them because they cared enough to be present in my darkness. They made a significant difference in my life and helped shape the person I am today, the beauty that came out of those ashes. I am also experiencing this with the friend I am supporting right now. There are three people who she was not close to prior to life kicking her in the gut repeatedly who have chosen to sit and sit some more with her (and by default they are also sitting with me as I support her). She now would call these friends key players in her life. In fact, when a birthday came around during this season of pain, when she was in no mood to celebrate, only these three were invited to be there with us. It was their willingness to be present that has made the difference and it has shaped the future of those relationships and the future of my friend's life.

Overall though, I have found that the authenticity required to actually pull this off requires a great deal of trust, which usually involves a great deal of history. The people I am willing to allow into my pain are the ones that have proven to love me for who I am regardless of my many flaws, who I have had to hash through relational problems with and still remain in relationship, and who I can laugh with. They are the people who can see me when I first wake up, before I've brushed my teeth, while my hair still looks like someone took a blow dryer to a llama just before he gets shaved. They are the ones who don't need my house to be clean, or my language to be clean for that matter. Because of the way they love me, I lean into their support when the page gets turned and I realize that the next chapter is going to be brutal. So now, twenty-plus years into my adult life, many of my painful chapters have the same characters and those characters are woven throughout my entire story in different capacities at different times.

Let me say though, that there are only about four of these characters who are consistent through time and one who is closest to me and my pain. This process of supporting someone through the valley is not for the weak of heart—it is painful and difficult, and often a much longer process than you think it should be.

What role do these characters play in my chapters of pain? They sit with me longer than anyone else. They are okay with the fact that three months after an emotional bruising from life I am still reeling, or that four years after a particularly brutal beating from life I still cry about the experience. They give me permission to feel pain without judgment about how I "should" feel or "should" be handling the situation at any given point in time. They teach me how to live in the new normal because they are by my side living it with me.

Who's to Blame (And Does It Matter)?

So far we have covered the first two lessons of helping hurting people. I'm not sure you need to take notes to remember what they are: just sit and sit some more—pretty basic. I hope though that you are getting the picture that what hurting people need is someone to be in the pain with them.

When It's Their Own Fault

What if the pain they are in is their own fault? Should the approach change? Should you sit with them while you tell them how their choices have gotten them into this mess? Should you sit some more and tell them they need to get their life straightened out or they will be in the same situation next year? When I ask in this way the answer is an obvious no, but in real life it is really hard not to handle things this way. Whether a person is responsible for their own pain or not the approach is the same: just sit and sit some more.

The need to have someone in the trenches with you is especially important when it is your own wrongdoing that has brought you there—this is not someone who is involved in the wrongdoing with you but someone who can ultimately pull you out of the muck. Probably the darkest time to date in my life came from my own wrongdoing. I already shared that my friend sat and listened to my confession and it was the kick off to the redemption process in my life. However, after my confession in her car, it took me months to actually get out of the muck and years before the pain of it subsided. She was present the whole time and her role changed over time but without her initial willingness to love me and be by my side even while I was drowning in my own wrongdoing I would never have believed that God could do the same. She did not approve of my wrongdoing, condone, or even accept it; she just loved me *in spite* of it.

Following my own experience of drowning in my own wrongdoing and paying the price in more ways than I ever thought possible, I had to go back and apologize to someone I loved for the way I had handled their wrongdoing. Someone in my family had an affair and the young children in the home were greatly affected by the outflow of all the consequences. The affair ended with the other party breaking things off and my loved one being brokenhearted over the loss of her family and the loss of this affair. In my anger at the time, I told her I was glad she was hurting from the break up because she deserved it. Yes, I actually said those words. I'm sure you can imagine how helpful that was to her in one of her darkest times.

What I later realized from my own experience is that we are all capable of *any* wrongdoing. "There but for the grace of God go I" is a saying for a reason—it is true. If you have gotten tripped up in wrongdoing in a way you never anticipated you will share my perspective. If you haven't I do not wish that on you. I do, however, think it is critical that you own the statement, "Given the right circumstances (or should I say the wrong circumstances) I am capable of any wrongdoing." If you do not believe that statement you cannot truly support someone being battered by the consequences of their own actions. You may not say the words I spoke to my loved one, but you will certainly think it.

The best example I can think of for this biblically is the woman caught in adultery. When the Pharisees bring her to Jesus, he has every right to stone her because of the law. Instead, he says to them all, "Let any one of you who is without sin be the first to throw a stone at her," which would make him the only one qualified to throw the first stone (John 8:7). But he didn't. He then says, "Neither do I condemn you" (John 8:11). If you know the story, he follows that up with "Go and sin no more." We will get to that part of this process but don't skip over his first response to her: He does not throw a stone when he rightfully could and then he tells her that he does not condemn her. You could not rightfully throw the first stone;

neither do you have the right to condemn someone else because of their own wrongdoing.

Let's not forget that we are the ones who place "levels" on wrongdoing—which Jesus abolished in the sermon on the mount when he said things like, "You have heard that it was said to the people long ago, 'You shall not murder, and anyone who murders will be subject to judgment.' But I tell you that anyone who is angry with a brother or sister will be subject to judgment" (Matt. 5:21–22). The point? Wrongdoing is wrongdoing. There are no "levels." Your wrongdoing is just as bad as the wrongdoing you think is worse. For me, harming your children because you had an affair was a worse wrongdoing than whatever daily wrongdoing I am forever involved with—gossip, pride, covetousness, etc.—and as such the offender deserved the punishment they got. That is not the way of Jesus. If you are going to be Jesus with skin on to a hurting person, you need to recognize that you are just as great a wrongdoer as they, and that "but for the grace of God" you would be in their shoes.

Being Jesus with skin on means you do not throw the first stone, and you do not condemn them for their wrongdoing. Then perhaps you will be given the opportunity to be the one that helps your loved one "go and sin no more."

When Someone Else Is to Blame

As I write this, I feel like this category is the worst, perhaps because of what my dear friend is presently going through. The pain humans cause each other is just unbearable. We see it on the news daily and we experience it in the lives of those we love more often than we care to count. If you are human and in relationships with others you will become a supporter to someone you love who has been wronged by someone else. It may be accidental or it may be deliberate but either way it is devastating.

I could give example after example of people I love who have been hurt by the wrongdoings of others. One of the hardest parts about supporting someone through this kind of pain is dealing with your own anger at the perpetrator and your own questions of how God could allow it to happen. When someone we love is wronged, let's be honest, we want revenge; we struggle with hate, anger, resentment, and on and on the list could go of all the negative emotions we have to deal with within ourselves while supporting the one who has been wronged.

Someone I love was raped when she was just thirteen years old, still very much a child. The perpetrator was a twenty-seven-year-old man from the church she attended who lured her into a secret sexual relationship. After a very long, drawn-out criminal court case, the perpetrator is in prison for statutory rape (among other charges associated with violation of a minor) and the scars remain on my loved one even now, more than ten years later. My most vivid memory of supporting my loved one through her dark time was a night we spent following a day in court laying in bed together while she cried and I cried and she told me stories about what she had been through. I did not say or do anything, I just sat with her; and then I sat next to her for a week during court and held her hand as she faced her perpetrator. Today, years later, when a bad dream wakes her up at night or a movie triggers her pain, she still calls me. The closeness of our relationship today is a direct result of that dark time in her life.

I still struggle with anger in regard to this situation and still have questions of how God could allow this to happen to an innocent. I still have no answers. But I see the woman she has become and the way she has become a survivor instead of a victim. All I have done for her over the years is be present when she needed me. Sure, I have said some things when she needed to hear them and I have been angry at the perpetrator and validated her feelings, but ultimately what she has needed most from me is for me to sit with her when she needs it.

Her pain is because someone else made a wrong choice. I can think of plenty of examples of when I was a victim of someone else's wrong choice and I could list story after story of close friends that have suffered because of someone else's wrong choice. I'm certain too that I have caused pain to others because of my own bad decisions.

The process for helping someone who is hurting because of the wrongdoing of another is the same: just sit with them and sit some more. Deal with your own anger and desire for revenge separately and allow them the space for their anger and confusion. Focus on how you can help your loved one directly instead of all the things you would like to do to the person who hurt them or to change the situation. When I have been the supporter in this kind of situation, I have found it helpful to get my own supporter to allow me the space I need to process through the pain I feel because of the harm done to my loved one; this has often been a friend, and even at times a counselor.

After someone has harmed you it is often those who care for you and protect you who restore your faith in humanity and give you a stable foundation to get your feet steady again. Be that kind of someone when your loved one is wronged by just sitting with them in the pain.

How Could God Let This Happen?

I think one of the most difficult questions to wrestle with about God is why bad things happen to good people. This is especially true when children are harmed but it also stands when someone you love is hit with a tragedy for which there is no explanation.

I have a dear friend who has chronic head pain. It began about ten years ago with no warning and no reason and has literally crippled her life. By chronic head pain, I mean imagine a migraine that never, ever goes away. She loves God and has been faithful in her pursuit of serving him with her life. She has lost her job, her home, her self-esteem, her relationships, and the ability to get through each day without severe pain. She has been to every head clinic and every natural doctor imaginable. She has tried acupuncture and narcotics. Nothing stops the pain for any significant period of time. She spends at least four days in the ER during a good month. This chronic pain is not the result of her wrongdoing or even the wrongdoing of someone else; it is the result of us living in a broken world, which basically means there is no explanation for it.

What's the first question we ask? Of course, it's "Why, God?": Why her? Why now? Why? Why? *Why?* My friend's response to that question? "Why *not* me?" It leaves me speechless that she can respond to her unexplained, incurable, chronic head pain in this way. I think she would tell you there are days she can say that and days that she still asks why and for how long but overall her response is amazing.

How do you support a loved one when there are no answers? The process is the same: just sit and sit some more. Don't pretend that there are answers. Don't go searching for hidden wrongdoing in their lives—God is not a punisher. Don't tell them it is God testing their faith or that this is a trial meant to refine them. You do not know what it is, so just say that. Just say you don't understand and you don't know why this is happening. Just sit with them, in the unexplained and potentially incurable pain. And for goodness sake, please do not say everything happens for a reason; that is just not true. I fully believe God can use any and every situation we go through to make us more like him and to impact the lives of others, but that is not the *reason* bad things happen; it is him being a God of redemption and healing. Bad things happen because we live in a broken world; there may just be no other *reason*.

What do you say to the parent who loses a child, or to the victim of cancer or a heart attack or chronic pain or illness, or the child diagnosed with leukemia? There are no answers. We live in a broken world. This is not what God intended for us. He created perfection in the Garden of Eden and we messed it up. There is evil in our world and because of that people suffer. It is no one's fault and there are no answers so stop trying to find them or act like you know them and just sit in the pain with your loved one.

Lesson 3: Show Up

This can be a challenging one. If you are someone who is naturally wired to do acts of service for those you love this will come more naturally to you but for those of you who are not (like me), trust me when I say that this can be learned! When someone you love is hurting you need to show up for those critical moments when they really need your support.

For me, this happened with a mentor who showed up every time I had to go to something that required me to deal with the pain I was in. She picked me up, took me, waited with me, and brought me home from each engagement. At the time I did not even remotely consider how challenging this must have been for her, as she was a professional with a full-time job, but she never mentioned it. Not being alone in these difficult moments is what made the difference for me and stopped me from sinking into the black hole I felt my life had become.

She also remembered the critical anniversary dates to this particular loss—at times even before I did. One of these stands out to me vividly: It had a been a year since life had flattened me and to be honest the date hadn't even registered to me yet, but she took the day off and told me she was coming to pick me up, no arguments allowed. We drove out to Starved Rock, a place to hike in the Chicagoland area. However, to add to the fun of the adventure she didn't get directions! She just wanted me in the car, safe and sound with her, while we went exploring. When we got to Starved Rock it was pouring—I'm talking, raining cats and dogs! We stopped at the gift shop, bought plastic ponchos and hiked until we were literally drenched. Upon leaving the park we stopped at Walmart, bought dry clothes and shoes and changed in the bathroom before hitting the Dairy Queen for the trip home. Her intentionality made what could have been a very difficult day for me something fun that I cherish remembering even now, many years later.

So what does this really entail, some grand notion or great plan? I hope my story indicates that there's little required beyond just showing up. My mentor just stuck me in a car and drove until we could breathe again outside of the city. It wouldn't have mattered what we did; I didn't have to be alone and I also wasn't forced to ask for help or admit my continued sadness one year after my life had been turned upside down. In fact, I would not have asked for help because I am, as previously mentioned, extraordinary at avoidance. I, therefore, would have acted like the date on the calendar didn't exist, and felt lousy all day without acknowledging why, which could have turned into many more days to follow of sadness and feeling alone. Sometimes we know what our loved ones need before they do, so show up for them.

Additionally, there are a lot of times that you will offer your presence to someone and they will decline your offer and say they are fine or they don't need anything. Here's my advice: If you have their address, show up anyway. Don't make it optional. And when you show up, remember that you don't have to talk about the pain; sometimes all they need is a ride in the car with a friend, a hike in the rain, a dinner out, a movie and popcorn, or watching some mindless TV with someone instead of by themselves. In fact, I would say most times, I just needed the distraction from my own thoughts and the reminder that I was not alone in the world.

One caveat here about learning this: it takes sacrifice. You will probably not want to go spend the day with your sad friend or sick family member. Do it anyway. I am a pretty active person—well, maybe it's better described as antsy: I don't sit still well. I prefer to spend my time busying myself being productive or going on some new life adventure. Hurting people just cannot handle that level of activity. Eventually, sure, you will want to pull them along on a fun adventure, but not for a while. First, you have to just show up. Put your own plans aside, put your own desires for how you would like to spend your day aside, and show up. Honestly, this was the hardest part for me to learn. I love being there for people and helping—of course, because I'm a social worker right? That is true...when it fits my schedule to do so. Just being honest here, this was really, really tough for me! To say to myself, "Boy, I would really like to hit the gym after work and go home to curl up with a book that makes me feel happy but instead I'm going to sit with my brokenhearted friend and let her cry and talk about the same situation she's been talking about for the last three months" was tough stuff! Initially, I tried just dragging them into my busy-ness. I felt like that was a good solution—they weren't alone and I still got to do what I wanted—turns out that's not a great plan. When you show up for someone, you put their needs above your own for that time; that is sacrifice and its required if you are going to show up for the people you love.

So, what changed for me, you ask? Someone made this sacrifice for me and it was invaluable to my well-being. This person never acted like she'd rather be somewhere else (though I'm sure there were many times that was true); she never told me about what she had cancelled or moved around in her busy schedule so that she could sit with me while I cried, or yelled (or let's be honest, acted like nothing was wrong); she just showed up for me. I learned to show up for people I love when they are hurting, even when they decline the invitation, because I know what it's like to have someone show up for me when I am hurting and the difference it makes.

Here's a little tip: use your calendar! When someone tells you about a court date, a doctor appointment, a counseling appointment, an anniversary date, any event that you know will be a trigger point for their pain, put the date in your calendar and set a reminder a few days before so that you can do whatever you need to in order to show up for that person. And remember that this is not about what you say, it's just about being present. You don't have the answers, you can't fix their pain, just show up for them and that will be enough for right now. We'll get into what to say when it's finally time to say something in the next few lessons.

Lesson 4: Choose Your Words

*O*kay, so after sitting, sitting some more, and showing up, you will have earned the opportunity to say some things. As with the other steps in this process, this took some learning for me. I am hopeful that for some people this comes naturally, but if you're like me, keep the faith!

Here's the issue I am up against with this idea of choosing my words. It's two things really: 1. I am an extrovert so I tend to speak before I think and end up inserting my foot into my mouth more times than I like to admit; and 2. I like to fix things; I want people to feel better so usually what comes out of my mouth first are potential solutions to the problem, whatever that might be. Bad plan.

Do *not* offer solutions. Trust me on this one, this does nothing but make your loved one feel worse. No matter how helpful you think you are being, and how clear your vision is because it's not happening to you, don't do it! So what can you say, you ask? Very little.

If I had to give you a few key phrases to memorize, here they are (short and sweet):

- "This is awful"
- "I can't imagine how you're feeling"
- "I am so sorry you are going through this"
- "Life can be so hard"
- "This must be terrible for you"

Are you getting the point? It is nothing but empathy, empathy, and more empathy. Now, as a side note, if you don't actually feel empathy this will be a major flop. You will come across as fake, because, well, you are being fake. You actually have to feel empathy for someone before you say something empathetic or it just comes out as patronizing.

A couple phrases to erase entirely from your vocabulary?

- "I know what you're going through": No matter how similar the situation is to something you have gone through, it is not the same so you *don't* know what they are going through.
- "I understand how you feel": No you don't! There's not much else to say about this, you just don't know how they feel because you are not them.

- "God won't give you more than you can handle": Ummm...way off on this one! This verse is in reference to God not giving us more *temptation* than we are able to resist and always providing a way out, not about suffering.

- "God works all things together for good": Yeah, not comforting in the slightest when you are hurting. Additionally, the words "for good" in this verse refer to making us more like him, not making our lives better.

- "Everything happens for a reason": No, everything happens because we live in a broken, dying world; there is no reason, it just happens.

I love how this plays out in the book of Job. Of course Job's whole world has been completely destroyed and his friends, in an attempt to comfort him, start rambling on and on instead of choosing their words. Here is Job's reply (Job 16:2–5):

2 I have heard many things like these; you are miserable comforters, all of you!

3 Will your long-winded speeches never end? What ails you that you keep on arguing?

4 I also could speak like you, if you were in my place; I could make fine speeches against you and shake my head at you.

5 But my mouth would encourage you; comfort from my lips would bring you relief.

I think you get the point. Niceties and quippy verses just don't cut it when life has kicked you in the gut. That being said, let's make it a given you do actually feel *empathetic*—tell them that—and only that...for now. You'll get your chance to offer truth and solutions but it's not time yet. The only thing that helps at this point is someone who loves you and knows you sitting with you, showing up, and "getting it." Do you get it? Do you know what it's like to be flattened by the pain of life?

Jesus did.

I love the story of Lazarus being raised from the dead. There are so many mysteries in this passage that connect to the way God handles prayer that I do not have the time (or the energy) to get into in this book; maybe in another one I'll tackle that. But in relationship to empathy this story gives us a perfectly clear picture of how Jesus handles the hurting people he loves.

When Jesus shows up after Lazarus has already been dead for three days, Mary runs to him crying, asking why he didn't come sooner and what does Jesus do? Say, "Mary, it will all be okay; I'm going raise him from the dead"? Nope. He just cries. "Jesus wept" (John 11:35). Shortest verse in the Bible (I'm sure you've heard of it). Jesus hurts because Mary hurts and he cries with her. He (unlike us) actually does know it is all going to be okay and that Lazarus will live again, but he tells her none of that. He just cries with her. He shows her empathy instead of speaking.

Go back to your Bible and read this story again through this lens. It is such a moving, intimate moment with Jesus and the hurting people he loves. He knows he has the power to stop the pain, and he will actually do that soon after this conversation (much later than they had hoped I might add) but it does not stop him from weeping with his loved ones because that is what they need from him in that moment. They need him to feel what they feel; that is empathy—he is hurting because they are hurting.

If you want to be Jesus with skin on to your loved ones you need to do the same. Choose your words. Don't just vomit out every word you can think of to try to make them feel better or fix the problem or change the subject because it's uncomfortable and you don't know exactly what to say; just be present in the moment of sadness, or anger, or hurt, or whatever it is, and feel what they feel.

Lesson 5: Speak Hope

*T*his can be extremely challenging when you do not know where to find hope in a terrible situation. As I write this I am currently struggling with this.

I am grasping at trying to find hope in this dying world where I see friend upon friend going through devastating circumstances. My dearest friend suffering because of someone else's actions, my friend with chronic head pain, another friend dealing with infertility and multiple miscarriages, another friend whose ten-week-old infant died, still another friend whose husband is absent in their marriage and offering no support; the list just goes on and on. This doesn't include what I hear from the clients I counsel on a daily basis. Life is hard. The older I get the more I realize how very unrelentingly hard it is.

I've talked about this earlier in regard to trusting in who God is when we cannot understand the what, how, or why of what he is or isn't doing. One thing I have learned to be true is that God NEVER does what I think he should, when I think he should, or how I think he should. Never. His ways are not our ways (Isa. 55:8). But he has made us promises we can stand on when life dumps us on our heads. His promises are the only place I have ever found hope in a horrific situation, in my own life, or in the life of someone I love.

Here is a journal entry that communicates my desire to cling to the hope I know to be true:

> In the brokenness that surrounds me
>
> I am forced to find hope
>
> Or be swallowed by despair
>
> There is too much pain and suffering
>
> In this dying world
>
> Too many questions of where You are
>
> And why You don't intervene when I think You should
>
> Then I remember
>
> That You never said You would
>
> Your promises are the only hope I know
>
> You have not left us here to suffer alone
>
> The pain around me is known intimately by You
>
> You know the number of hairs on my head

And collect my tears in a bottle

You weep in my sadness

Even when You know the ultimate outcome

You are here

Here with me

Here with the broken and the hurting and the dying

You are here

You…

Are Hope

Some of God's Promises

Here are just a few of the specific promises I have learned to cling to:

- Who he is never changes (Heb. 13:8).
- He will never leave us (Deut. 31:6).
- He cares for us (1 Pet. 5:7).
- He knows the number of hairs on our heads (Mat. 10:30).
- He will sustain and rescue us (Isa. 46:4).
- He has given us the Holy Spirit as our comforter and peace (John 14:26–27).

- He knows us intimately (Jer. 1:5).

- He has overcome the world (John 16:33).

- He can relate to our pain in his humanity (Luke 22:44).

- He is bigger than we can ever imagine and sees much more than we can (Job 38).

- He is our redeemer (Isa. 54:5).

- We have been bought with a price (1 Cor. 6:20).

- He gives us peace that goes beyond understanding (Phil. 4:7).

- Nothing we do can separate us from his love (Rom. 8:38–39).

If you can think of other promises (for there are certainly pages and pages of them) take a moment to jot them in the margins.

Once you have identified where you find hope, it is time to speak it into the life of your loved one.

At this point you have earned the right to speak truth. They know that you are okay with wherever they are because you have sat with them in the pain; they know your desire is to support them because you have shown up for them; they know you do not think the words you use are quick answers or feel-better statements because they have experienced your empathy—now is when words of truth actually mean something to them. The same rules apply as before—these cannot be quippy verses or phrases that you don't have any experience clinging to; they must be real to you, you must truly believe them or be honestly seeking to cling to them in your doubt. I think it's the genuineness that you bring with your words that makes the difference.

At this point, in the situation my dear friend is going through, all I can say in honesty is that God has not forgotten her, he is with her, and he is still ultimately on the throne. That's it. That's all I have that is genuine at this point; even though I believe all the promises I listed above, these are the only three truths that have truly settled into my anxious heart and given me hope for her in what seems to be a hopeless situation.

Additionally, I speak the truth of the situation to her. We all know what it is when our perspective of a situation does not match the reality of the situation because of the pain it is causing us. Your thoughts greatly impact—no, let me state that stronger: your thoughts *determine* your emotions.

Here is a silly example of a time when I learned the power of my thoughts: As a recent college grad I played in competitive volleyball leagues. I spent high school and college playing on an indoor court but the leagues I played in were primarily in the sand. I am not a huge sand person, in general. At the beach I like things sand free and find it annoying when the sand blows onto my blanket or someone shakes a towel out and the sand ends up sticking to my suntan oil (seriously, why must people shake out their towels around those tanning). Needless to say, you spend quite a bit of time in contact with the sand when playing sand volleyball. So, during a game when I was busy complaining about getting sand everywhere one of my teammates said, "That's it! Every time you hit the sand I want to hear you say, 'I love the sand'!" No joke, I started to do it. Unbelievably, over the course of time, without even recognizing it, my feelings about playing in the sand changed. I actually loved the sand and played in leagues for years following that, preferring the sand over indoor court volleyball. We underestimate the power of our thoughts.

In the professional world of counseling this is called cognitive behavioral therapy. In the world of supporting a loved one, I call this "telling yourself the truth." In my own dark hour, my mentor would force me to tell her (yes, out loud) five of the promises I knew to be true. For my friend at this time I am forcing her to tell herself the truth of what is happening in her circumstances by repeating certain true statements out loud to me. Here are a few examples (in addition to the promises above) I might ask someone to repeat after me, until they actually believe it (a lot like "I love the sand" but much more important):

- My value is not based on what others think of me.

- God has not forgotten me.

- The truth will not change.

- I will make it through this.

- God has not left me, he is with me.

- The decision the other person made is about them, not about me.

- Nothing can separate me from the love of God.

- I'm important and valuable.

- I am forgiven.

- Who I am is not defined by this circumstance.

Notice that some of these are based on specific verses of scripture and others are nuggets of truth based on reality. If they cannot say these things to themselves you need to say it to them—repeatedly. The truth needs to settle in to their broken heart because that is where hope is born—out of truth.

Speaking truth into the life the brokenhearted is a key component in the restoration process. They most likely do not feel the presence of God and their vision is so clouded by pain they have lost sight of his promises and the truth of the situation. That is why God uses people in our lives to be Jesus with skin on. We are responsible to remind our hurting loved ones of the hope promised to us by the God who loves us. We cannot promise that everything will be okay, or that it will all work out, but we can promise that he is present with them in the pain; they are not alone, and you are the tangible picture that allows them to cling to the hope that that promise could actually be true.

Do you see that you are the physical manifestation of his promises in their darkest hour? It is because of your unconditional love, support, and presence that they can believe that God is still who he said he was before their world fell apart and that he is still with them. Slowly, they will begin to actually feel the presence of God again in their life.

Just a reminder, this is the fifth step in the process of helping the hurting. With the friend I am supporting, who has a very strong faith, it took five months to get to the point where she could even hear these words, much less start to allow them to settle into her wounded spirit. Make sure the timing is right when you speak truth.

Final Lesson

So, I hope you've gotten a grasp of the steps to helping the hurting. These are by no means exhaustive but in my experience they have proven to be the five most critical components to helping someone you love who is hurting. The final question I think you may be asking is how do I know when I go to the next step of support? Is there a time frame for all of this?

The answer: Nope. There is no time frame; no guarantees that if you do this all perfectly your loved one will bounce back or not get mad at you for doing the wrong thing at the wrong time. This is not a "fix it" formula. It's more of an intentional mindset you carry with you throughout your life and in your relationships. For some people these steps will be cyclical; for some they will progress quickly. One painful situation may go completely different than another painful situation for the same person; there is nothing for sure beyond the fact that they need you.

When you handle it wrong or say the wrong thing, just apologize. That's it. Don't make excuses or get upset that they got mad when you were only trying to help. Remember how badly they are hurting and tell them you are sorry and it was never your intent to cause them more hurt or frustration. You may ask them what they need most from you at any given time but honestly, the reason I wrote this is that most people have no idea what they need when they are distraught, so you will be left to figure that out; my intention is that this book will help you do that.

Remember that your own emotions will play into this whole process as well. As I mentioned, right now I am very much struggling with clinging to the hope of Gods promises. I have forced myself to move toward that struggle because it is what my friend needs. I am brokenhearted for her and my own doubt and anger is in play here. I don't hide this from her but I cannot add my pain to what she already carries. This is the burden that comes with true empathy, there is no way around it. Instead, you must be intentional about seeking out your own support system. For me, this has come through seeing a professional counselor and staying connected with a couple close friends that I can be authentic with. But because your emotions are involved, you are more likely to do or say something that is not necessarily helpful; if you have been sitting with them, showing up, and giving empathy to them they will forgive quickly. It is those steps that earn you the right to speak into the life of your loved one, which also earns you the right to do it wrong sometimes and receive forgiveness for it.

In Closing…

I wish I could tie all this up in a pretty bow. But when it comes to pain in life, there just are no bows. My closing thoughts come from what I am going through right now in supporting someone I love:

Hang in there. Cling to the hope you know exists in the person of Jesus Christ and the fact that he does not change like the shifting shadows (James 1:17). I find the conversation between Job and God in the book of Job so encouraging in times when I feel swallowed up by the pain this life brings. I have taken the liberty of removing a couple verses but have left the references for your information. In Job 38, the conversation between God and Job begins:

[1]Then the Lord spoke to Job out of the storm. He said:

[4] "Where were you when I laid the earth's foundation? Tell me, if you understand.

[5]Who marked off its dimensions? Surely you know! Who stretched a measuring line across it?

[6]On what were its footings set, or who laid its cornerstone—

⁷while the morning stars sang together and all the angels shouted for joy?

⁸ "Who shut up the sea behind doors when it burst forth from the womb,

⁹when I made the clouds its garment and wrapped it in thick darkness,

¹⁰ when I fixed limits for it and set its doors and bars in place,

¹¹ when I said, 'This far you may come and no farther; here is where your proud waves halt'?

¹² "Have you ever given orders to the morning, or shown the dawn its place,

¹³ that it might take the earth by the edges and shake the wicked out of it?

¹⁴ The earth takes shape like clay under a seal; its features stand out like those of a garment.

¹⁵ The wicked are denied their light, and their upraised arm is broken.

¹⁶ "Have you journeyed to the springs of the sea or walked in the recesses of the deep?

¹⁷ Have the gates of death been shown to you? Have you seen the gates of the deepest darkness?

¹⁸ Have you comprehended the vast expanses of the earth? Tell me, if you know all this.

¹⁹ "What is the way to the abode of light? And where does darkness reside?

²⁰Can you take them to their places?
Do you know the paths to their dwellings?

²¹ Surely you know, for you were already born! You have lived so many years!

²² "Have you entered the storehouses of the snow or seen the storehouses of the hail,

²³ which I reserve for times of trouble, for days of war and battle?

²⁴ What is the way to the place where the lightning is dispersed, or the place where the east winds are scattered over the earth?

²⁵ Who cuts a channel for the torrents of rain, and a path for the thunderstorm,

²⁶to water a land where no one lives, an uninhabited desert,

²⁷to satisfy a desolate wasteland
and make it sprout with grass?

²⁸Does the rain have a father?
Who fathers the drops of dew?

²⁹ From whose womb comes the ice? Who gives birth to the frost from the heavens

³⁰ when the waters become hard as stone, when the surface of the deep is frozen?

³¹"Can you bind the chains of the Pleiades? Can you loosen Orion's belt?

³² Can you bring forth the constellations in their seasons or lead out the Bear with its cubs?

³³Do you know the laws of the heavens? Can you set up God's dominion over the earth?

³⁴ "Can you raise your voice to the clouds and cover yourself with a flood of water?

³⁵ Do you send the lightning bolts on their way? Do they report to you, 'Here we are'?

³⁶ Who gives the ibis wisdom or gives the rooster understanding?

³⁷ Who has the wisdom to count the clouds? Who can tip over the water jars of the heavens

³⁸ when the dust becomes hard and the clods of earth stick together?

³⁹ "Do you hunt the prey for the lioness and satisfy the hunger of the lions

⁴⁰ when they crouch in their dens or lie in wait in a thicket?

⁴¹ Who provides food for the raven when its young cry out to God and wander about for lack of food?

God continues on for a few more chapters listing all the things Job cannot contend with. I love this because I think God just gives Job a reality check (lovingly of course), and he is even sarcastic as he does it (38:21: "Surely you know, for you were already born! You have lived so many years!"). I love this because it is exactly the kind of reality check I need when I am drowning in the pain of life to remind me that I am not sovereign and I am not in control but that God is. The NIV begins chapter 38: "then the Lord speaks to Job out of the storm"; the NASB and ESV start, "then the Lord answered Job out of the whirlwind." It is during the storm, within the whirlwind that God reminds Job of his ultimate power. He does not fix anything, or change anything; he just reminds Job of who he is. I need that reminder during these storms too.

Here is another passage I cling to (Psalm 46:1–7):

1 God is our refuge and strength, an ever-present help in trouble.

2 Therefore we will not fear, though the earth give way and the mountains fall into the heart of the sea,

3 though its waters roar and foam and the mountains quake with their surging.

4 There is a river whose streams make glad the city of God, the holy place where the Most High dwells.

5 God is within her, she will not fall; God will help her at break of day.

6 Nations are in uproar, kingdoms fall; he lifts his voice, the earth melts.

7 The Lord Almighty is with us; the God of Jacob is our fortress."

It is the only hope I know to offer you and your loved ones when the storms of life send you flailing. Cling to the character of the God who made your loved one and loves them even more than you can ever imagine. Your job is not to fix anything or change the circumstances, that is all on God and his sovereignty. You job is to be Jesus with skin on during the darkest hours of someone you love: just sit, sit some more, show up, choose your words, and speak hope.

About the Author

Cori Moschberger is a Licensed Clinical Social Worker. She has been in the field of social services since 1998. She received her Master of Social Work from the University of Illinois at Chicago in 2003.

Cori is a clinical therapist and an organizational development consultant and trainer residing in the northwest suburbs of Chicago. She is a dog lover, enjoys new experiences, especially adventures, but still makes time to "just sit" and care for others.

As a consultant and trainer, Cori specializes in the not-for-profit sector. Her expertise includes management, team building, leadership, and mentoring.

As a clinical therapist, Cori uses a strengths-based approach with all her clients. She creates a safe and comforting environment that allows clients to discover their strengths in order to live happier and more enriched lives.

www.ingramcontent.com/pod-product-compliance
Lightning Source LLC
Chambersburg PA
CBHW031427040426
42444CB00006B/725